POSITIVE STEPS

Respecting Others

by Susan Martineau

with illustrations by Hel James

A⁺

Smart Apple Media

Published by Smart Apple Media
P.O. Box 3263, Mankato, Minnesota 56002

Printed in the United States of America at Corporate Graphics,
in North Mankato, Minnesota.

Library of Congress Cataloging-in-Publication Data
Martineau, Susan.
 Respecting others / by Susan Martineau ; with illustrations by Hel James.
    p. cm. -- (Positive steps)
 Includes index.
 ISBN 978-1-59920-493-2 (library binding)
 1. Respect for persons--Juvenile literature. 2. Etiquette for children
and teenagers--Juvenile literature. I. James, Hel. II. Title.
 BJ1533.R42M37 2012
 179'.9--dc22
                                                    2011000251

Created by Appleseed Editions, Ltd.
Designed and illustrated by Hel James
Edited by Mary-Jane Wilkins
Picture research by Su Alexander

Picture credits
All photographs from Shutterstock.
Contents page Zurijeta; 4 Gelpi; 5 Vinicius Tupinamba 6 Dmitriy Shironosov;
7l Ivan Pavlisko, r Forster Forest; 9 Benis Arapovic; 11t Mandy Godbehear,
b John Steel; 12 Monkey Business Images; 13 Beata Becla; 14 Morgan Lane
Photography; 15 Zurijeta; 16 (main image) Bluefox; (inset) Zurijeta; 17t Monkey
Business Images, b Hirurg, background Hal_P; 19 Fotoksa; 20 StockLite; 21 AXL;
22 Alexander Chaikin; 23t ZQFotography, bl Wawritto, br Tischenko Irina;
24 Sklep Spozywczy; 26 Filip Fuxa; 27l Dmitriy Shironosov, r SergiyN;
28-29 Iakov Kalinin; 32 Margot Petrowski
Cover: Forster Forest/Shutterstock

DAD0048
3-2011

9 8 7 6 5 4 3 2 1

Contents

Thinking of Others

When we treat people respectfully, we show that we care about how they feel. The things we say or do make a difference to other people. We need to treat our friends, family, and other people the same way as we would like them to treat us.

Be kind to other people.

We need to be careful about how we talk to other people and how we listen to them. **Polite** words such as "please" and "thank you" are important, but how you say and do things also matter. You can even have an argument with someone in a respectful way!

Listen to other people's point of view.

Look at what these children are saying. They are talking about some ways of showing respect to other people. Can you think of any more? Look through the book to see some examples.

Show respect to everyone, not just your friends.

Think of ways you can help other people.

Treating people respectfully shows that we have thought about what they need and how they are feeling.

Please and Thank You

Being polite to other people is an important way of showing respect to them. Having good **manners** helps everyone get along with one another.

Greeting our friends shows them we care for them and how they are feeling. When we ask for something at school, at home, or in a store, it is good manners to say "please." Don't forget to say "thank you" too!

We should always thank someone when we've been at their house or if they gave us a present.

Sometimes we also need to be able to say "no" politely. We will not sound **rude** as long as we say, "No, thank you!"

Thank you for having me.

Thanks for the awesome present.

Design a Card

There are times when you cannot thank someone in person. You could design your own thank you card. It could be one to send in the mail or one to e-mail.

Thank you

The present is great!

THANKS MOM

Making Friends

Anna has just moved to a new town far from her old home. She is writing to her best friend Jasmine.

Hi Jas,

The new house is great and I love my bedroom, but I'm missing you a lot. I'm really worried about starting at my new school next week.

What if I don't make any friends or they don't like me? I'm so scared.

Write soon. Wish you were here.

Love Anna

confused

lonely

excited

nervous

shy

sad

lost

How could you help Anna if she was coming to your school? Look at the words on the left. Do they describe how you felt on your first day of school?

What can you do?

If you notice someone looking lost and lonely you could:

- Go and say "Hi." Ask them their name.

- Invite them to join in a game.

- Offer to sit with them at lunchtime.

- Help them find their way around.

Can you think of any other ways to be **kind** and show respect to a new person?

I've made lots of new friends.

Listening to Others

When we listen politely to other people, we show them that we respect them and want to hear what they are saying. When we meet someone new, we need to listen to them so we can find out about them and get to know them.

Hi, I'm Aaron. What's your name?

I'm Jack.

Do you like soccer?

We should not forget old friends too! They also need to know we are interested in what they say and do and that we care about how they are feeling.

Listening politely to grown-ups is very important. They might be telling you something that will keep you safe.

LET'S TALK ABOUT . . .

How do you know if someone is really listening to you? Look at the list below and see if you can think of anything else.

They let you finish what you are saying without **interrupting** you.

They look you in the eye when you are talking.

They ask you questions about what you've just said.

The Listening Game

Everyone gets into pairs with someone they do not usually talk to or play with. Ask each other questions about your favorite games, food, or movies. Then take turns to **introduce** your partner to the others.

This is Oakley. He's seven years old. His favorite food is pizza!

11

Can I Help You?

Helping at school or at home shows that we are thinking about other people. Being **considerate** like this means we are not just thinking about ourselves. We are respecting others.

Try to be tidy at home and don't leave your stuff lying around for other people to clean up. Offer to put the groceries away or help with the laundry. Maybe you can help cook too.

What can you do?

At school you could offer to pick up the classroom or help hand out books and other things for your teacher.

When we are out and about, we also need to think about how our actions make a difference to others. We should always wait our turn in line and hold the door open for people behind us.

How I helped on

Monday   put laundry away

Tuesday   cleaned my room

Wednesday

Thursday

Friday

Saturday

Sunday

The Helping Diary

You could keep a diary of all the things you've done to help at home or at school during the week. Maybe you could even persuade your teacher or family that you deserve a treat when you show them the diary!

It's Party Time!

Ben is feeling a bit hurt because he was not invited to a party. He is writing to his older cousin about it.

Hi Josh,

How are you? I'm OK but I didn't get invited to Ethan's party last week. He told me he was sorry, but his mom said he couldn't invite the whole class.

Look forward to seeing you soon.

Ben

Respecting others means thinking about their feelings, but sometimes it is hard to keep everyone happy. Can you think of a way that Ethan could cheer Ben up? Maybe he could invite Ben over to play another time?

What can you do?

If you are having a party, remember to think of other people's feelings. If you can't invite everyone, try not to give out invitations at school in front of everyone. Don't talk about your party in front of anyone you have not invited!

Please Don't Slurp

Table manners might sound boring, but they do matter. If we eat politely instead of grabbing food or eating with our mouths open, it makes meal times nicer for everyone. It shows we respect the other people at the table.

LET'S TALK ABOUT . . .

Can you think of times when it's all right to use your hands to eat? Some countries have different ways of eating. For example, in China and Japan, people eat food with chopsticks.

The Eating Game

Ask your parents if you can practice setting the table with knives, forks, and spoons. Take turns sitting down and eating some imaginary food! You could try this eating game with chopsticks too.

When you eat at a friend's house, it is polite to thank them for the meal. Try to eat the food you are given even if you do not like all of it!

Having an Argument

You stupid idiot!

We all lose our tempers from time to time. We sometimes **disagree** with our friends or don't want to do things their way.

Shouting or being rude to someone is **disrespectful**. **Swearing** and name-calling are also disrespectful.

I'm sorry, but I don't really agree with you.

You can disagree with other people in a **calm** and polite way. Then they are also much more likely to listen to your point of view. Try the game on the next page to practice this.

LET'S TALK ABOUT . . .

How do you feel if someone shouts or yells at you? You are likely to shout back and then everyone gets even more upset. Can you think of other words to use in a polite argument?

I see what you mean, but . . .

Yes, but what about . . .

Don't laugh at what someone says unless they are making a joke.

The Debate Game

Take turns talking about swearing. Why do people swear? Is it ever all right to use swear words? Each speaker has a minute to talk and then everyone else can ask them questions.

Listen to each speaker without interrupting.

Speak clearly and politely.

Try to Be on Time

Being on time, or being **punctual**, shows good manners and that we respect others. Nobody likes to be kept waiting.

We should always try to be on time, whether we are meeting friends or going to the dentist.

*If you are late and keep others waiting, it is like saying that your time is more important than theirs. It is **selfish** and **inconsiderate**. Can you think of times when you have had to wait for someone? How did it make you feel?*

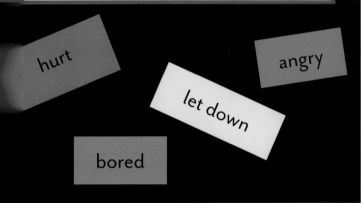

hurt

angry

let down

bored

What can you do?

Take **responsibility** for being on time. Perhaps you could ask for an alarm clock to help you wake up in the morning. When you get ready to meet someone or go to school, keep an eye on the clock or a watch to check that you are going to be punctual.

Don't Litter!

Please don't drop that. Someone else will have to pick it up.

No one likes to see trash lying on the ground. Old chip bags, candy wrappers, and empty soda cans are **litter**. Litter is dirty and unhealthy, and it belongs in the trash can!

If we throw our trash on the ground, it means we do not respect or care about other people or our **environment**.

What can you do?

Check where the trash cans are in your school. Does everyone know where they are? Maybe you could ask your teacher about **recycling** some of the things you throw away at school. Cardboard and paper can all be recycled. This is good for our environment.

Don't Chuck It, Can It!

You could design some posters to put up that remind everyone that they should put their trash in the can!

PAPER

PLASTIC

CANS

Just Can It!

On the Phone

Hello?

Hello, Anya. Could I speak to your mom please?

When we are on the phone we need to speak clearly and listen carefully. Anya is answering the phone at home.

Anya needs to find out who is calling. She can write down the person's number so her mom can call back.

She can't come to the phone at the moment. Can I take a message?

If someone grunts "yeah" or "what?" on the phone it sounds rude! Can you think of some good ways of answering the phone? Remember that you do not have to say your name unless you know the person who is calling. Can you also think of polite things to say when you are making a phone call?

Hello, who's calling please?

Who would you like to speak to?

Hello, could I please speak to Dan?

Hello, it's Holly. Is Martha there please?

Can I Take a Message?

Play this phone game with as many people as possible. One person "calls" another and asks if they will pass on a message. The second person then has to "call" someone else and pass on the same message. Keep going until you run out of people and see if the message has been passed on correctly!

Having Visitors

When our friends or family come to visit us, it is good to make them feel welcome by showing them that we are pleased to see them.

Hello, Uncle Jim. How are you?

Do you want to come and see my new hamster?

Even if they have come to see everyone else in the house, we should not ignore them or just keep watching TV when they arrive.

Try to think of something your visitor might like to do.

What can you do?

Visitors will feel at home if you:

- Greet them when they arrive.

- Talk to them and ask them what they would like to do.

- Ask them if they would like something to eat or drink.

When visitors are about to leave, say goodbye to them so that they know you enjoyed seeing them.

Being Respectful

Being respectful to others means you care about the way you treat them and you care about what they think of you. There are many ways to be respectful.

Don't be a litter bug!

Be welcoming to visitors or new people.

Sometimes other people are not very respectful toward us. We should still try our best to be respectful toward them.

Be thoughtful and kind.

Respect others as you would like them to respect you.

Look at people when they are talking to you.

What can you do?
Look at the bold words in the book. Check that you know what they mean by turning to the glossary on pages 30–31. Get into pairs and make up some sentences using the words. Write your sentences on a separate piece of paper. Remember to listen to each other!

The **bold** words are explained on pages 30–31.

Speak to people politely.

Being punctual is polite.
If someone is rude, stay calm!
Respect helps us all to get along.

Take responsibility for being on time.

Glossary

calm
quiet; not noisy or excited

considerate
thinking about what other people would like and about other people's feelings

disagree
to not agree with someone; to think they are wrong

disrespectful
not showing someone respect and not being considerate

environment
the world around us

inconsiderate
not thinking about others or their feelings; the opposite of considerate

interrupt
to speak when someone else is talking

introduce
to tell others someone's name and something about them so they can get to know them

kind
friendly, considerate, and helpful

litter
trash that has been thrown on the ground

manners
Having good manners means saying "please," "thank you," and "sorry."

polite
having good manners

punctual
being on time

recycling
making trash into things that can be used again

responsibility
Taking responsibility means being in charge of something yourself.

rude
having bad manners and not being polite

selfish
thinking only about yourself and not about others in the way you behave

swearing
using rude words that might upset people

Web Sites

13 Basic Table Manners for Kids
http://www.drdaveanddee.com/elbows.html

Crawford the Cat Videos: Please and Thank You
http://www.crawfordthecat.com/video/index_011.html

Library Thinkquest: Values Index: Respect
http://library.thinkquest.org/J001709/thinkquest_
values/2respect/respect_frameset.html

Hello, how are you?

I see what you mean, but . . .

Listen carefully.

Put it in the trash can.

Index

Friends care about each other.

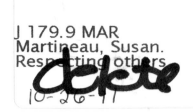